AuthorHouse™ UK
1663 Liberty Drive
Bloomington, IN 47403  USA
www.authorhouse.co.uk
UK TFN: 0800 0148641 (Toll Free inside the UK)
UK Local: 02036 956322 (+44 20 3695 6322 from outside the UK)

Because of the dynamic nature of the Internet, any web addresses or links contained in this book may have changed
since publication and may no longer be valid. The views expressed in this work are solely those of the author and do
not necessarily reflect the views of the publisher, and the publisher hereby disclaims any responsibility for them.

Any people depicted in stock imagery provided by Getty Images are models,
and such images are being used for illustrative purposes only.
Certain stock imagery © Getty Images.

This book is printed on acid-free paper.

ISBN: 979-8-8230-8383-6 (sc)
ISBN: 979-8-8230-8384-3 (e)

Print information available on the last page.

Published by AuthorHouse 07/24/2023

authorHOUSE®

# To all MY dearest little ones

# Milda Tilly B.

# my dearest little one

## Illustrated by author

My dearest little one,
I know you are fragile and scared
'Cause the world out there can be very
Daunting and unpredictable.

You may not know what is around the corner.

You may not know what the future will provide.

My dearest little one,

No one knows about the future or what is ahead.

We may not know what our plans are.
What are our roles? Where are the instructions?
Where do we begin, or where do we end?
Who will we meet, or where will our homes be?

No, I cannot tell what will happen
Today or tomorrow.
But I can tell you this: You will definitely
Have a memorable and incredible journey!

And don't be scared, my little one!
You will never be alone on this journey.
You will meet new and unique little creatures.
As unique as you and I.

Yes, they are unique: Do you know why?
Because we are all different!
But you will have a very special union,
A union that is also called friendship.

No matter how different we are,
Our differences won't necessarily separate us.
They can still bring us close,
No matter how different we are.

Our friends are part of our journeys.
My dearest little one,
Imagine a world without them.
Imagine a journey without them.

Be brave, my dearest little one,
Be brave!
You are stronger than your fears.
You have friends to meet and so much to learn!

Trust me ...
You will meet the ones who are brave.
They will teach you how to take
Every step with courage!

Trust me ...
You will meet the ones who are strong.
They will teach you how to handle
Every challenge with resilience!

Trust me ...
You will meet the ones who are wise.
They will teach you that
knowledge is a bright light

Which shines through the darkest moments!

Trust me ...
You will meet the ones who
are vulnerable.
They will teach you how to be
strong for them

And to show enormous compassion.

Trust me ...
You will meet the ones who are weak.
They will teach you to move on and remain
Compassionate without losing dignity.

Our friends may teach us a lot,
But we are also part of their journeys too!
We may be their teachers.
We may also be their heroes!

We have priceless gifts, inspiring each other,
Accepting each other, listening and seeing.
Nurturing and understanding,
Loving unconditionally!

My dearest little one, do not trade love!
Every kind gesture will be rewarded.

Be proud of a loving heart.
Be proud of being noble.

There will be moments in your journey,
My dearest little one,
When you will feel defeated,
Exhausted, and lonely.

My dearest little one, remember
Every journey has some rough roads,
Has sad moments.
But they won't last; I promise you they won't last.

Every night ends with a dawn,
And every daylight ends with a night.
Every sunshine ends with rain,
And every rain ends with bright skies.

So don't be afraid, my dearest little one.
Rough journey roads won't last long.
Everything is balanced,
Everything has a start and an end.

Be brave as a soldier,
My dearest little one!
Be humble and noble,
Loving and patient!

Now imagine, my little one,
A land or a world
Where everyone is forgiven,
and everyone is loved.
Where finally, everyone
feels like it's home.

It may sound impossible,
But we can make it together!
We want this journey to be meaningful;
We want to bring a new season!

I trust you, my dearest
little one,
'Cause we are here for a reason,
And that reason may or may not
be clear:
It's important to be brave.

I trust you, my dearest little one,
'Cause you will not fear the challenges ahead!
Your courage is your power;
Your patience is your armour.

I trust you, my dearest little one.
Whatever we will face,
It is for us to grow and learn.
Be resilient and calm in the storms ahead.

Oh my dearest little one,
You are so much loved.
Be that shining light through the dark.
Be that shining light from heart to heart.

Come! Your journey is ahead of you.
My dearest little one,
The world can be daunting and unpredictable,
But your courage and patience,
Love and compassion,
Unique friends,
Will make this world a better one!

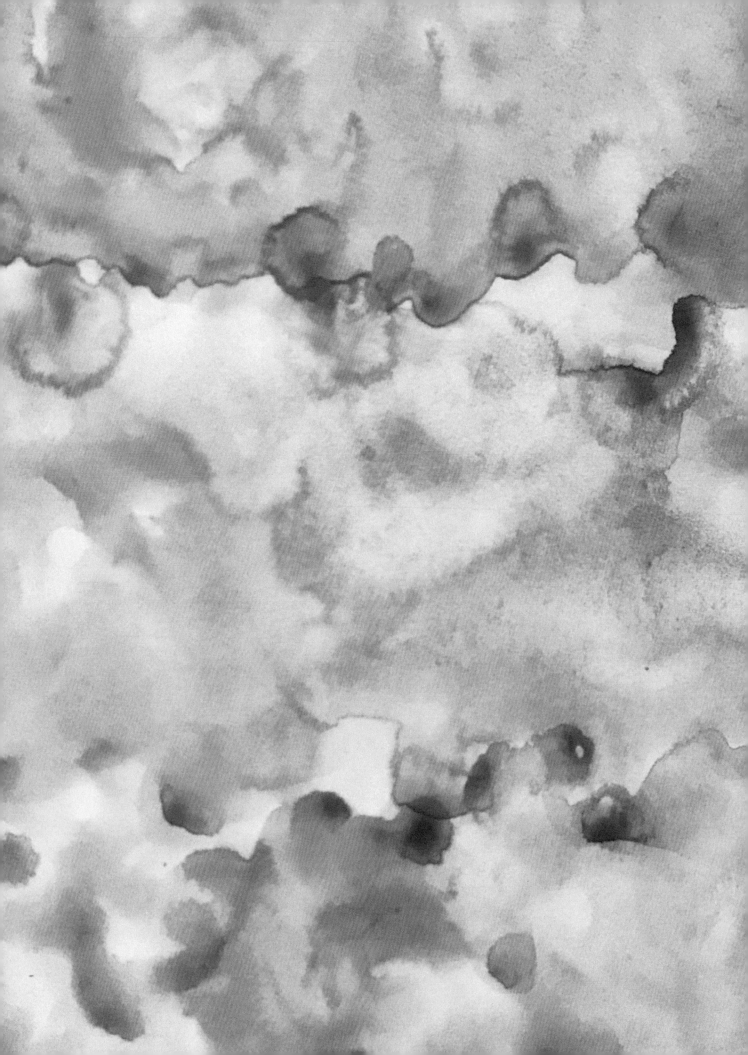

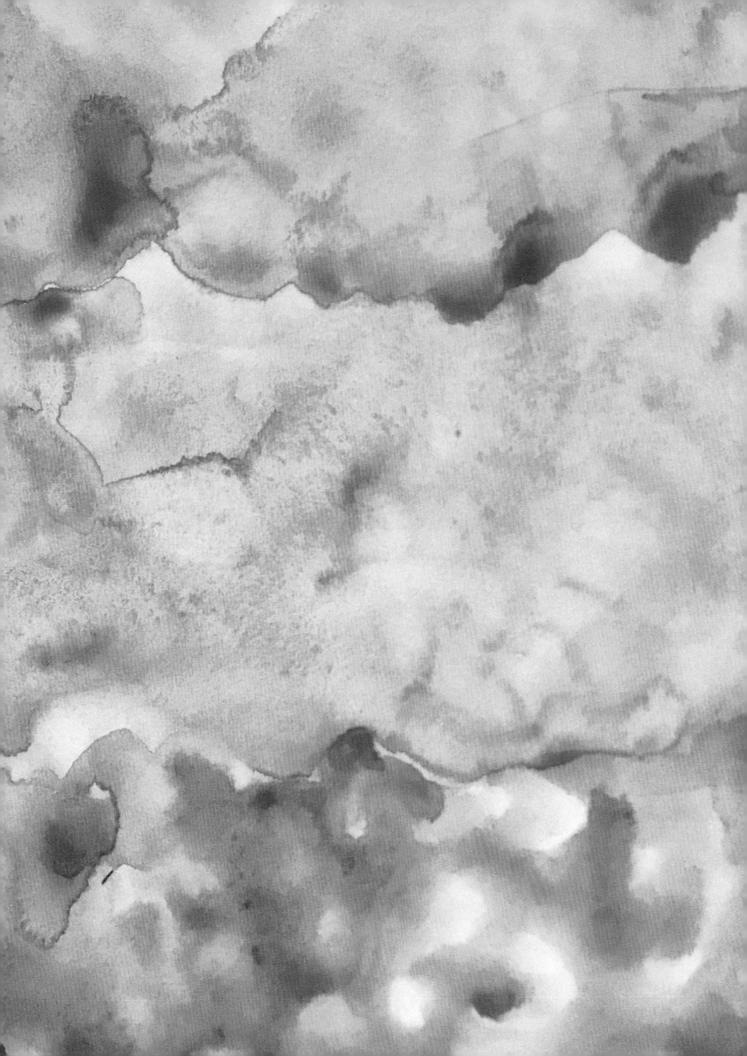

Printed in the United States
by Baker & Taylor Publisher Services